Thoughts of
PEACE

FREDERICK LEE

Review and Herald Publishing Association
Washington, D.C.

CONTENTS

The Quest for Peace of Mind

WE LIVE in an era of growing tension. The tempo of modern life is not conducive to rest and relaxation, and man is afflicted with many lurking fears and uncertainties that our forefathers never knew. This is partly because man's little community has been widened to take in the whole world. Daily he hears of happenings in lands across the seas—a riot in one country, a war or a revolution somewhere else, disagreement at an arms limitation conference. And he is made to feel that these things sooner or later will most certainly affect his security and peace.

Besides concern for these things abroad he feels the impact of changes that are taking place all about him. Nothing seems to be stable. Government, business, labor, society—all are being affected by revolutionary ideas. We are told that most of man's inner conflicts come from his feeling of insecurity. No wonder then that one writer states that modern man is "stricken by psychic anxieties, cloven by emotional conflicts, beset by economic insecurities, assailed by political doubts and cynicisms."

The growing quest for peace of mind is a most significant phase of modern life. This is evidenced in the large number of books and magazine articles on this subject appearing in recent years. A cursory glance at best-seller nonfiction books indicates a definite trend in this direction. Such titles as *Peace of Mind, How to Stop Worrying and Start Living, Making Our Minds Behave, How Sane Are You? A Guide to Confident Living, Road to Sur-*

vival, Peace of Soul, The Mature Mind, Don't Be Afraid, reveal a widespread desire for tranquillity and inner peace in these uncertain and chaotic times. The increasing number of people seeking psychiatric treatment is another evidence of general unrest in the souls of men.

If man is to have peace, he must have something to make him feel both important and secure. One cannot by only a word say to his fears, "Begone," and then find release. He needs to know that there is One greater than himself who cares, upon whom he can call for help that will not fail. He needs a refuge sure and steadfast to which he can go for shelter. This is no flight from reality, no escape from the issues of life. It is rather the finding of solid ground upon which to stand and face life with courage when all about is only shifting sand.

The reason so many men and women are filled with inner fears today is that they have lost touch with God. They have been left stranded and alone in a cold and uncertain world. They have been told that if there is a God, He could not possibly be concerned with their personal affairs. The modern concept of God is that He is One who started life and then withdrew, leaving things to work out by the law of the survival of the fittest. But such a belief is little comfort in days like these.

We are glad for the experience that David left on record in the Psalms. Here we find just the message needed for these bewildering times. David too was driven to despair by circumstances. He was frustrated in his attempt to appease an unstable king. He was hunted like a wild beast and betrayed by friends. He became the king of Israel, but he was tempted, and sinned as any common man. His life seemed to be a succession of victories and defeats. He often fell deep into the pit of despair. Sometimes it was because of the way wicked men seemed to prosper. Again it was because he was treated unjustly. At other times it was because of his own sins. What did he do on such occasions? He had one remedy that proved to be infallible, and he availed himself of it again and again.

Over and over we see these words in the Psalms in one form or another: "Trust in the Lord," "Wait upon the Lord." In the thirty-seventh psalm we find this sequence, which we believe reveals God's formula as well as David's for a distraught mind.

"Fret not thyself."
    "Trust in the Lord."
        "Commit thy way unto the Lord."
            "Rest in the Lord."
                "Wait patiently for Him."

The key words are "trust" and "wait." Trust is an absolute and unquestioning resting on that which is its object. The object in which we trust or upon which we lean must be of such power and stability as to hold our confidence at all times. Unless we have such a God as that, we have no God at all. We must not err on the grounds of placing God so far away that He cannot help us, nor make Him so limited that He cannot be concerned with our individual needs. You must believe, as one has fittingly said, that "God gives Himself in loving attendance to you as if you were the only person in the universe."

Trusting God, we commit our cares and problems to Him. And then we wait upon Him. The trusting-waiting process is that which calms the soul and rids us of lurking fears. It brings us into conformity with God's will, and we say, God's way is always best.

To wait on God is the test of trusting in God. To trust presupposes a waiting time. Life's problems cannot always be solved immediately. It is the lingering problems that cause us the greatest distress. Those who have learned to wait on God have found a way to carry such burdens and not break under them. Sometimes the waiting must be long, and God's answer to our call may be deferred.

At such a time we must remember, also, that God may have a better plan than that for which we plead. And some may have to die waiting, as did Abraham, who died in faith not having received the promise, and came to be called the father of the faithful; or as did Moses, who longed to enter the Promised Land but was sent out to die on the barren hills of Moab instead—and awoke in Paradise!

There is no better remedy for our inner anxieties and conflicts than to trust in God and wait also on Him. Furthermore, in such a formula for life there is greater good to be found than merely present release. Through it we find redeeming grace, and by it we are bound to eternity. Well may we exclaim, "O Lord of

5

hosts, blessed is the man that trusteth in thee." And when we do trust in Him, peace like a river refreshes our souls.

> "Give to the winds thy fears,
>   Hope and be undismayed;
> God hears thy sighs and counts thy tears,
>   He shall lift up thy head.
>
> "Through waves, and clouds, and storms,
>   He gently clears thy way;
> Wait thou his time, so shall this night
>   Soon end in joyous day.
>
> "Leave to his sovereign sway
>   To choose and to command;
> So shalt thou, wondering, own his way,
>   How wise, how strong, his hand!
>
> "Far, far above thy thought
>   His counsel shall appear
> When fully he the work hath wrought
>   That caused thy needless fear."
>   —PAUL GERHARDT

The True Guide to Peace

THE Bible speaks directly to this present troubled world. Its great outstanding message is concerning peace. If you would find true foundations for peace of mind, turn its pages, memorize its promises, study its prophecies, heed its teachings, and contemplate its revelation of God.

Peace of mind is the measure of our preparation for life. It is not a peace that comes apart from God. It is that peace which comes through communion with God.

The great purpose of the Bible is revealed in these words of Christ: "These things I have spoken unto you, that in me ye might have peace. In the world ye shall have tribulation: but be of good cheer; I have overcome the world." John 16:33. "Peace I leave with you, my peace I give unto you: not as the world giveth, give I unto you. Let not your heart be troubled, neither let it be afraid." John 14:27.

Here is peace that is different from that which the world gives. It is Christ's peace. This is not a peace that is subject to the changing and uncertain pattern of life, the whims and fancies of men, or even the rise and fall of nations. As Christ is the same yesterday, today, and forever, so is the peace He gives. To have our peace in Him is to have fellowship with Him and to be surrendered to His will. He takes the lead, and we follow Him. Just as long as we are conscious of walking in His steps, what have we to fear?

Here is a sure way of peace, more certain than the counsels of men. Every true principle of mental health is enunciated in the Scriptures. In the words of prophets, priests, apostles, and of the Master Teacher Himself we find that which men and women need today for consolation and peace of mind. Note this testimony of the prophet Jeremiah written in a day of great darkness and gloom:

"Thy words were found, and I did eat them; and thy word was unto me the joy and rejoicing of my heart."

Jeremiah was a prophet of doom and lamentation. He had to speak much of destruction and despair, of affliction and woe. And he had to bear the penalty and stigma of such a role. His people turned from him. The king demanded that he keep silent, and thrust him into prison. His messages were burned. Who wants to hear the voice of judgment? No doubt the burden to warn a wayward people and to give rebuke cut deep into the prophet's character. His, it would seem, was not a happy lot.

Of his day the prophet wrote, "We looked for peace, but no good came; and for a time of health, and behold trouble!" Jeremiah 8:15. What a familiar picture of our own time these words present. We too live in a day of judgment. Agents of God today are warning of coming doom. Bible predictions are daily being fulfilled.

Yet amid these premonitions of evil and calamity we may find words of comfort and love. Should we not dwell upon these messages of hope from God more than we do? How much we need words of encouragement and assurance in a day like this, when so many Jeremiahs are marching up and down the land, crying, "Woe, woe, woe unto the inhabitants of the earth!"

The Word of God is not a doomsday book only. It is a treasure house of good things that will fill our days with peace and happiness. Of this word Job declared, "I have esteemed the words of his mouth more than my necessary food" (Job 23:12), and Israel sang, "How sweet are thy words unto my taste! yea, sweeter than honey to my mouth!" Psalm 119:103.

The Bible is pictured as a great table spread with appetizing food. All we need do is to search and find that which will be most refreshing to our taste. God's words of assurance, of present and future hope, apply to any situation in which we may find ourselves. What do you long for most as regards spiritual need? You will find it among the delicacies spread out in the pages of Scripture.

True, you will find words there that are tart and bitter, but you need not feed continually on these things. How much there is in the Word of God that reveals His goodness and His love, His care and protection! Let us daily partake of that which will give us joy.

But we must *search* for these words. Jeremiah says, "Thy words were found." This indicates that it took some seeking. How often as we read through the Bible we seem to find much that depresses and perplexes. Then suddenly we come across a verse that refreshes and gives us comfort and strength. All through the Scriptures are scattered these choice morsels of spiritual food.

Jeremiah said that when he found the words he ate them. By that he meant that he did not merely nibble at them, take them up, put them to his lips, and then lay them down again. No, he took them into his very soul. He assimilated them. He meditated upon them until they were a part of himself. It was then that they became the joy and rejoicing of his heart.

How often in partaking of food we do not know its good flavor because we do not take time to masticate it long enough. It is the same with God's Word. We must take time to meditate upon it, think of its deepest implications and its personal application. Too often we think of God's Word as spoken to people in general, and forget that it is like a personal message to each child of faith.

Let us partake more of the refreshing spiritual food to be found in the Bible. Let us not think on that only which is unpleasant and causes us distress. Let us, with Jeremiah, who was called to speak so much of calamity and affliction, search for the many words of life and health that are to be found in the messages that God has sent to us.

It is such words as found in the following scriptural quotations that we should meditate upon in these days of uncertainty:

"For the mountains shall depart, and the hills be removed; but my kindness shall not depart from thee, neither shall the covenant of my peace be removed, saith the Lord that hath mercy on thee." Isaiah 54:10.

"Yea, I have loved thee with an everlasting love: therefore with lovingkindness have I drawn thee." Jeremiah 31:3.

"The Lord is good, a strong hold in the day of trouble; and

9

he knoweth them that trust in him." Nahum 1:7.

"Come now, and let us reason together, saith the Lord: though your sins be as scarlet, they shall be as white as snow; though they be red like crimson, they shall be as wool." Isaiah 1:18.

"Bless the Lord, O my soul, and forget not all his benefits: . . . who satisfieth thy mouth with good things; so that thy youth is renewed like the eagle's." Psalm 103:2-5.

"Behold, I create new heavens and a new earth: and the former shall not be remembered, nor come into mind. But be ye glad and rejoice for ever in that which I create." Isaiah 65:17, 18.

These are words which are the source of our peace and happiness in a day of trouble. There are more like them all through the Bible. Let us search them out and dwell often upon them. They will be as the wise man said of pleasant words, "sweet to the soul, and health to the bones." Proverbs 16:24.

No wonder David exclaimed in spite of his many hard experiences, "O taste and see that the Lord is good!" Yes, let us taste, and we shall see!

You Are Not Alone

THE feeling of being forgotten is not a healthy one. The sense of belonging is absolutely necessary to man's well-being. One cannot live alone, detached as it were from the stream of life, and develop a well-rounded character. We are dependent on the love, the thoughtfulness, the consideration, and the understanding of others. Man was created a gregarious creature. God said of him, "It is not good that the man should be alone." Therefore man reaches his greatest satisfaction when he is part of a group wherein are mutual love and sympathy. This, of course, is realized to the best and fullest extent in the Christian home.

But there is a larger fellowship than that of the home. It is found in the church. Here the scope of one's relationships is enlarged and raised to a spiritual plane. Christ declared of the one who lost father, mother, brother, or sister for His sake that he would be rewarded in this life with "brethren and sisters, and mothers, and children," in the fellowship of the church.

There is a still higher and even closer relationship than these. It is the tie that binds us to God. The sense of belonging to an all-wise, long-suffering, merciful heavenly Father, who knows and understands our joys and sorrows, is more valuable to man's mental, physical, and spiritual well-being than anything else. The reason for this is that God never fails to know and understand. He is never absent from us. And He is the same yesterday, to-day, and forever.

The golden chain that binds the hearts of loved ones is often

11

broken. The family circle tends to disintegrate. Even those of the same religious communion may find it hard to understand us. In fact, it is not always possible for another human being to understand our deepest longings, because it is not often possible for us to express them. But with God we need not even attempt to tell Him how we feel. He knows even before we utter a word, and knows far better than if He were dependent on our telling Him. How wonderful is this thought to troubled minds!

Loneliness can be as painful as a disease and as disastrous to mental and physical health. It comes most often as the result of the loss of or separation from loved ones. But it also comes as the result of unfulfilled desires and ambitions, or through estrangement and misunderstanding.

Whatever the cause, there is one universal cure. It is found in the words, "God knows and understands." The Bible was written to give us this assurance. Man was not cast off from God's interest when he sinned, though he was cast out of Eden. God has gone to great pains to make us understand this. He went so far as to send His Son into the world to live with men, bear their sorrows, and die with them.

Christ, the Son of God, felt the bitter mental pain of loneliness. It was said of Him that He trod the winepress alone, and of the people there was none with Him. (Isaiah 63:3.) In Gethsemane's dark hour, when it would have been good to feel the sympathy of understanding friends, He was compelled to say to those who were supposed to be closest to Him, "What, could ye not watch with me one hour?"

The Son of God was overlooked by the great of earth, and even the leaders of His own nation passed Him by. "He was despised and rejected of men." How little we know of the homesickness, the heart longing, that was felt by the Master. Only now and then did He feel the satisfaction of being among those who truly understood and loved Him. On the cross He had to pass through the experience of feeling that God had forgotten Him.

Christ went through all this that He might know how to help and comfort those who for one reason or another have the feeling of being alone and forgotten. The very fact that He did this is the greatest evidence that we are not forgotten.

There is much in the Word of God that emphasizes God's personal concern for and interest in the individuals who live in this world. God understands our needs.

Of Abraham He said, "I know him, that he will command his children and his household after him." Genesis 18:19.

To Moses He said, "Thou hast found grace in my sight, and I know thee by name." Exodus 33:17.

Concerning his son Joseph, Jacob said, "The arms of his hands were made strong by the hands of the mighty God of Jacob." Genesis 49:24.

Job declared, "But he knoweth the way that I take: when he hath tried me, I shall come forth as gold." Job 23:10.

In the vision of John, God said to each of the seven churches, "I know thy . . . tribulation, and poverty." And to another, "I know thy . . . charity, and service, and faith." Revelation 2:19.

Surely there is sufficient in the Scripture record to make us know that we are not forgotten. Friends may not know. Loved ones may not understand. We may be forgotten as far as the world is concerned. But God knows and cares.

How, then, are we to relate ourselves to the problems of life that so often trouble us and cause real worry? Two words are sufficient for an answer—surrender and trust. A surrendered heart and a trustful spirit are greater than any change of circumstances that may come to one. The spirit is stronger than the body, and a spirit strengthened by the almighty arm of God is one that cannot be overwhelmed!

The consciousness of living according to the divine will, along with a faith in the mercy and justice of God, will do more to calm the troubled heart and bring rest to the fearful mind than all the words of wisdom of men. Indeed, what real harm can come to the one who trusts in God?

> "Just leave in His dear hand
>   Little things;
> All we cannot understand,
>   All that stings.
> Just let Him take the care
>   Sorely pressing,
> Finding all we let Him bear
>   Changed to blessing."

Oh, let us cherish the blessed truth that God knows and cares, and let us never, never allow ourselves to become distraught because of some discouraging experience or seeming neglect. Friend, cast all your burdens on the Lord, ''for he careth for you.'' 1 Peter 5:7.

HE LEADETH ME

''In pastures green?—Not always; sometimes He
Who knoweth best, in kindness leadeth me
In weary ways where heavy shadows be.
Out of the sunshine, warm and soft and bright,
Out of the sunshine, into darkest night;
I oft would faint with sorrow and affright.

''Only for this: I know He holds my hand;
So, whether in a green or desert land,
I trust, although I may not understand.
And by still waters?—No, not always so;
Ofttimes the heavy tempests round me blow,
And o'er my soul the waves and billows go.

''But when the storm beats loudest, and I cry
Aloud for help, the Master standeth by,
And whispers to my soul, ''Lo, it is I.''
Above the tempest wild I hear Him say,
''Beyond this darkness lies the perfect day;
In every path of thine I lead the way.''
So whether on the hilltops high and fair
I dwell, or in the sunless valleys where
The shadows lie, what matter? He is there.

''And more than this: where'er the pathways lead,
He gives to me no helpless, broken reed;
But His own hand, sufficient for my need.
So where He leads me I may safely go;
And in the blest hereafter I shall know
Why in His wisdom He had led me so.''

—*Selected*

14

Begin With God

AS JESUS stood one day on Mount Olivet looking over Jerusalem, the beloved city, His soul was stirred with deep emotion. He thought of the false strivings of His people after righteousness and peace. He thought of the fears that often assailed them. He looked into the future and saw that they would have sufficient cause for fear. How He longed to help them. With what tenderness He cried out. "O that thou hadst known in this thy day, even thou, the things which belong unto thy peace!" Luke 19:42, A.R.V., margin.

When His people are disturbed and distraught Jesus is troubled. He longs for the peace of those who follow Him. He does not hold Himself aloof from man, but is ever seeking some way to deliver him from his afflictions. In these words we note how great is His concern, and how earnestly He longs to help those who face great trials.

But what can He do when the people refuse to let Him help them? It was this that caused His anguish of heart. He came unto His own to deliver them, but His own received Him not. He knew that this very rejection would increase their sorrows. They might boldly cry, "His blood be on us, and on our children," but how little they knew of the terrible consequences of those words. To the women who followed Him as they "bewailed and lamented him," He said, "Weep not for me, but weep for yourselves, and for your children." Luke 23:28.

What are the things which belong unto our peace? First and

foremost is our relationship to God. This is the foundation of peace.

We are receiving a generous amount of advice these days on how we can obtain peace of mind. Too much of this advice starts off in the wrong direction. If anyone has the idea that man can get along quite well without God, let him note the state of the world since men have been trying to do this. Has it not been dinned into the ears of man for a hundred years that where once God ruled, science was ready to take over? Let God pay attention to the other worlds. We could get along very well without Him. Some who once felt this way have now repented as they see the dire results of such teaching.

It is true in the world, it is true with every individual, that life begins with God. We are connected with God by the very act of creation, and by His continued sustenance. What then is the status of that relationship? This is the great question for those who are seeking untroubled thoughts. Let this relationship to God first be settled, and all other problems will fall into their proper setting; indeed, this very act will cause many problems to vanish. Then we can fearlessly say, "If God be for us, who can be against us?"

Here is what Paul says in regard to this: "Therefore being justified by faith, we have peace with God through our Lord Jesus Christ." Romans 5:1. The Bible speaks of a reconciliation that must be made. "Be ye reconciled to God," urges the apostle. It is not God who needs to be reconciled to man. He never was estranged from man. It is man who separated himself from his Creator, and broke the connection with the Source of life. Now man must return, as illustrated in the parable of the prodigal son, and make reconciliation with his heavenly Father. The provision has been made whereby this can be brought about. All man needs to do is to accept the good offices of the chief Advocate, Jesus Christ, to make things right with God. All sins against the mercy and love of God will be forgiven and blotted out, and one can walk forth with the consciousness that all is well.

"Peace with God." Little do we realize, as we go about our usual duties from day to day, how much that means. But let some great trial come, one that no man can help us solve—perhaps it is facing death itself—then the great question arises: "What is a man profited, if he shall gain the whole world, and lose his own soul?" We might paraphrase these words thus: What shall it profit a man to make peace with all his problems by some source of power he may discover within himself, and then find when the final word is about to be spoken that he has overlooked the greatest issue of life, one that determines his eternal destiny, peace with God? Then it is that the anxieties over material things and the way someone has treated us, which have taken so much of our attention, will seem very small; and we will realize that, above all else, our relationship to God has more to do with our daily and eternal peace than anything else.

To have peace with God would immediately solve many of our inner conflicts that result in worry and anxiety. There is no better illustration of this than the very personal record Paul left for us. Note what he says:

"For I know that in me (that is, in my flesh,) dwelleth no good thing: for to will is present with me; but how to perform that which is good I find not. For the good that I would I do not: but the evil which I would not, that I do. Now if I do that I would not, it is no more I that do it, but sin that dwelleth in me." Romans 7:18-20.

A war was going on in Paul's life between the "law in my members" and "the law of my mind," as he described it. The flesh cried out, "Do it." The conscience answered, "Be careful. Watch your step. This may lead to your moral downfall. And this is never worth while." And yet the call of his members was so strong that time and again he found it shouting down the urgings of his conscience. No wonder he exclaimed, as we all do at times, "O wretched man that I am! who shall deliver me?"

Too many today are going to the wrong source for deliverance. You may read all the books on how to stop worrying, and try to stamp out anxiety by substitution of something pleasant, but this is not the answer for people who consciously are going contrary to the will of God. Their deliverance can be found only where Paul found his—in the Lord Jesus Christ.

After the stormy chapter of Romans 7, how restful it is to begin reading the eighth chapter of this epistle.

"There is therefore now no condemnation to them which are in Christ Jesus, who walk not after the flesh, but after the Spirit.

. . . For what the law could not do, in that it was weak through the flesh, God sending his own Son in the likeness of sinful flesh, and for sin, condemned sin in the flesh: that the righteousness of the law might be fulfilled in us, who walk not after the flesh, but after the Spirit.'' Romans 8:1-4.

The restless spirit of that great man at last found peace, but it was a calmness of soul that was brought about through reconciliation with his God.

There are many things that belong to our peace, but let us not, in our searching, neglect the weightiest question of all: Have I found peace with God?

Mastering Your Fears

THERE probably never has been an age when men generally were so full of fears as now. The more we come to depend on the accumulation of material things for happiness, the more complicated life becomes, and the more fears seem to assail us. This is a strange consequence of progress. But it is a fact of life today that gives the leaders of men no little concern.

One noted writer has said:

"The great scourge of mankind is not war, though it is frequently referred to as such. It is something much more fundamental—something that plays its part in producing wars. It is fear —an emotion tremendously devastating to the human personality. There are people who begin the day with fear. It is their constant companion through all their waking hours, and it is beside their bed at night."

This writer states that there are two kinds of fear: one, the constructive kind that is definite and about which we can immediately do something; the other, the imagined fear that is not attached to any particular object. Some menace seems to haunt the person thus afflicted. He becomes overanxious in every situation in which he finds himself. This is an unnatural fear, for which there may be several causes. One cause may be some physical ailment that needs attention. But more often these fears develop because of some destructive emotion that has taken hold upon the mind, such as resentment, hate, or jealousy. Then too, these lurking fears may come because of some repressed sense of guilt, resulting from unconfessed wrongdoing.

The thing one must do is to try to discover the reason for such fears and do something about them, such as confessing a wrongdoing and seeking forgiveness, or casting aside the troublesome and unreasonable resentment that may be ruining one's peace of mind. The point that needs to be emphasized is that we must do something about our fears, not dwell on them. When we have done all we can to make matters right we should shut our minds to the things that have been troubling us. If at some time or another our former fears come knocking on our doors, we must not let them in.

When there is a healthy spiritual experience these mental ills to which humanity is subject will not have such a hold on us. Paul tells us, "God hath not given us the spirit of fear; but of power, and of love, and of a sound mind." 2 Timothy 1:7. We must link ourselves to these spiritual resources. When, through the grace of Christ, the mind has been cleansed of the fears that have troubled us so long, we must fill the vacated place with thoughts of love and faith, and set up a watchtower against the evils that once possessed us. As we move forward in active service under God, doing good perhaps to those who once distressed us, seeking spiritual power to overcome natural weaknesses, and trusting God to settle all questions we cannot solve, we will find that our fears completely vanish.

The Christian should have a sound mind, one that is not weakened by inner conflicts but free to think upon those things which upbuild and make one strong. We are told that "he that feareth is not made perfect in love." 1 John 4:18.

Love is a selfless quality. It is objective. Fear is a self-centered quality. It is subjective. Dwelling too much upon self, thinking of one's weaknesses, one's failings, and the things that have made us ill or caused us distress tend to create fears within us. Love puts us to work for someone else. We are preoccupied with thoughts about God, our loved ones, our friends, and others who may need our ministrations. We have little time to think of self. Then it is that we are most free from fears.

The spirit of fear has no part in Christian experience. The goodness of God leads us to repentance. His love holds us true to principle. Though justice will have its place, yet God emphasizes His mercy and long-suffering to bring us to terms with Him. He declares, "With lovingkindness have I drawn thee." Jeremiah 31:3.

The term *fear,* used so much in connection with God, means reverence and awe, not dread. He holds no threat of torment over our heads to bring us to our knees. No, He does it by a supreme sacrifice of His best and dearest, the sacrifice of His only begotten Son.

Fear has no place in the Christian category of words. It is a usurper in the camp of Israel. Peace is the gift of God. But fear is the poison that the enemy would pour into the soul of man.

No wonder, then, that on one occasion when the disciples revealed great anxiety over their own safety, expressing surprise, Christ said, "Why are ye so fearful?" What matter the stormy sea, the high wind, the rocking boat? Was He not in their midst? Had He not bidden them follow Him? Why would they not trust Him? Had they not confessed that He was the Son of God? Had they not seen the miracles that He had performed? "How is it that ye have no faith?" He asked.

Yes, it is something unreasonable for the Christian to have fears. They come only from a lack of faith. If Christ is near, and we are Christ's, what can truly harm us? It is with this reasoning that we should face our fears. Let the light of faith shine into all those dark corners of the heart and the mind to drive away the gloom lurking there.

Consider this encouraging counsel:

"For the disheartened there is a sure remedy,—faith, prayer, work. Faith and activity will impart assurance and satisfaction that will increase day by day. Are you tempted to give way to feelings of anxious foreboding or utter despondency? In the darkest days, when appearances seem most forbidding, fear not. Have faith in God. He knows your need. He has all power. His infinite love and compassion never weary. Fear not that He will fail of fulfilling His promise. He is eternal truth. Never will He change the covenant He has made with those who love Him. And He will bestow upon His faithful servants the measure of efficiency that their need demands."—*Prophets and Kings,* pp. 164, 165.

We must not think that we should be free from the assault of fears. It is natural and normal to fear certain things. No one is a coward because of this, or needs to go down in defeat. As one has well said, "It is what we do with our fears that counts. Only when we allow them to dominate us are we vanquished. . . . Courage is not the absence of fear but the conquest of fear."

When Paul spoke of a sound mind he referred to a healthy, self-disciplined mind, one that is held in subjection to high purposes and a calm trust in God. The consciousness of divine aid fortifies the mind, and fits us to meet all life's problems.

"Wherefore take unto you the whole armour of God, that ye may be able to withstand in the evil day, and having done all, to stand." Ephesians 6:13.

There is no better advice anywhere than this for the troubled soul of man. When we have committed our ways to God and have done all we know how to do to face the issues before us, then let us stand unwaveringly and await the outcome. Say to yourself without fear, "Let the blow fall if it will. I trust in God." It will surprise you how often the thing that you fear will never come to pass. It may be that for some reason or other you have exaggerated the issue. Or it may be that God has turned aside the blow. And then again it is likely that even though the blow was great you survived the ordeal better than you imagined you would.

The message of God to us is: "Be not afraid nor dismayed by reason of this great multitude; for the battle is not your's, but God's. . . . Ye shall not need to fight in this battle: set yourselves, stand ye still, and see the salvation of the Lord." 2 Chronicles 20:15-17.

The one who is traveling with Christ, as the disciples were on stormy Galilee, need have no overwhelming fears. To all such He says, "Peace, be still."

"LORD, TAKE AWAY PAIN"

"The cry of man's anguish went up unto God:
    'Lord, take away pain—
The shadow that darkens the world thou hast made;
    The close-coiling chain
That strangles the heart; the burden that weighs
    On the wings that would soar—
Lord, take away pain from the world thou hast made,
    That it love thee the more!'

Then answered the Lord to the cry of the world:
    'Shall I take away pain,
And with it the power of the soul to endure,
    Made strong by the strain?
Shall I take away pity, that knits heart to heart,
    And sacrifice high?
Will ye lose all your heroes that lift from the fire
    White brows to the sky?
Shall I take away love, that redeems with a price,
    And smiles at its loss?
Can ye spare from your lives that would climb unto
    mine,
The Christ on his cross?' ''

—Found on the wall of a Denver hospital.

Good Medicine for the Troubled

THERE are many man-made formulas for peace of mind, but none is so effective as the command of God to be thankful. Paul in writing to the church at Colosse encouraged the believers with these words:

"Let the peace of God rule in your hearts, to the which also ye are called in one body; and be ye thankful." Colossians 3:15.

Once a year in the United States the President sets aside a day for thanksgiving. He calls upon the people of the nation, as he did in a recent proclamation, to consider "the richness of our blessings," "our bountiful harvests," "our productivity of goods abundant," and the privilege "to walk as free men unafraid." It is good to remind ourselves of such things once a year. But it is far better to set a time each day to ponder the things for which we should be thankful.

The spirit of thankfulness is like a tonic. It causes one to lift his head, to walk more erect. It smooths the ruffled brow, and places a smile upon the countenance. "Nothing tends more to promote health of body and of soul than does a spirit of gratitude and praise."

Thus we are admonished by the prophet Samuel, "Consider how great things he hath done for you" (1 Samuel 12:24); and our hearts should respond as did the psalmist, "The Lord hath done great things for us; whereof we are glad." Psalm 126:3.

Just the uttering of praise and thanks sends the blood coursing through one's veins faster, cleansing out the impurities of the mind and the heart, and giving health to the bones.

Again we are told, "It is a positive duty to resist melancholy, discontented thoughts and feelings,—as much a duty as it is to pray."—*Ministry of Healing,* p. 251.

Certainly we have much to be troubled about, for there never was a time when so many demands were made upon us. Life becomes more and more complicated and uncertain every day. We seem to be hedged about by unpleasant events over which we have no control. We often feel disconcerted in the face of issues that must be settled without delay. How can we remain calm and collected in such a time as this?

The best way to do it is to have a background of confidence that we have an Almighty Helper at our side every moment, and that He will not permit any circumstance to overwhelm us. We need constantly to remind ourselves of this, and be thankful for it. This is what Paul meant when he wrote the words quoted before. Weymouth's translation reads:

"Let the peace which Christ gives settle all questionings in your hearts, to which peace indeed you were called as belonging to His one Body; and be thankful." Colossians 3:15.

The consciousness that we are not alone in the daily conflict, that we belong to a body of people who are called to peace through Christ, tempers every trial and helps to settle all our questionings. This is one of the greatest blessings that the Christian way of life has to offer. We not only look forward to the day of salvation, when we shall be delivered wholly from earthly conflicts, but we are promised daily deliverances here and now. That is why Christ bade us pray, "Deliver us from evil." This freedom comes not by its removal, for this is impossible in an evil world, but by God's making evil powerless over us, even as rain is repelled by a waterproof garment. We can then say with Paul, "None of these things move me."

How thankful we should be for these spiritual blessings that moderate the trials of life. And the more we are thankful for them, the more they can do for us. Of this we read:

"It is for our own benefit to keep every gift of God fresh in our memory. By this means faith is strengthened to claim and to receive more and more. There is greater encouragement for us in the least blessing we ourselves receive from God than in all the accounts we can read of the faith and experience of others. The soul that responds to the grace of God shall be like a watered garden. His health shall spring forth speedily; his light shall rise in obscurity, and the glory of the Lord shall be seen upon him."— *The Desire of Ages,* p. 348.

When we think of our material blessings we may not have as much as some for which to be thankful. We may be poor in this world's goods; we may have afflictions of the body and be restricted in our activities. It may seem, as we compare ourselves with others, that we have little to call forth thankfulness. But all have the same access to the storehouse of heaven, and we are only limited by our faith in laying hold of the spiritual blessings God so freely offers to all. If it is money you need, God can bless the little and make it sufficient. If it is health you need, God can give you the grace to endure the trial. There is no material need of man that some spiritual grace cannot match. Just take the key of faith and open God's treasury, and there you will find all that is necessary for a life of happiness. Help yourself to the riches of joy and gladness stored up in Christ Jesus.

There are two ways to multiply our blessings. One is to recognize them. The other is to share them. This is an axiom of life in general, and of Christian life in particular. To let money lie idle in a bank often defeats one's purpose. But to put it into circulation, and let it produce something useful to others, is the best way to increase one's own benefits. This law of economics is recognized in the business world. It was recognized by Christ in the parable of the talents. The man who buried his one talent in the ground, thinking he would have wherewith to meet some future need, learned to his great regret that even that which he had felt was so secure was taken from him.

Exaggerated self-interest leads sooner or later either to poverty of material things or poverty of soul. What, then, should be the response of one to every blessing that is received? "Freely ye have received," saith the Master, "freely give." And the psalmist asks, "What shall I render unto the Lord for all his benefits?" There is no peace for one who simply offers thanks for what he receives. He must likewise be glad for the opportunity to serve. To give is life; to stop giving is death. To Abraham, God said, "I will bless thee, . . . and thou shalt be a blessing." The one who stops being a blessing will soon lose the blessing.

There are too many people today talking about the Bill of Rights and forgetting the bill of responsibilities. We love our freedom to do as we wish. But does what we wish include the desire to be of some help to others? No nation, no people, no individual, would have any freedom at all if no consideration were given to human relationships.

Above all, spiritual life is absolutely dependent upon the act of sharing. One concerned only with his own salvation is doing the very thing that will keep him from receiving what he desires.

So let us be thankful for the faith that helps us lay hold upon the eternal riches, for the hope that keeps us patient until we fully realize all that God has promised, and for the love that prompts us to give thanks for blessings bestowed and leads us to share them with others. This is the way of peace to which we are called. Let us walk in it.

Finding a Sure Refuge

IN GENESIS 7 we read these words: "The Lord said unto Noah, Come thou and all thy house into the ark." "And Noah went in, and his sons, and his wife, and his sons' wives with him, into the ark," "as God had commanded him: *and the Lord shut him in.*"

What wonderful assurance it must have given that little group of faithful ones to know that God's hand was on the door that shut them in! What feelings of security and repose that knowledge must have given them when the lightning flashed and the thunder rolled and the first storm ever unleashed upon humanity burst over them in all its fury and terror.

Have you ever felt the cheer and relaxation of entering a lighted room, warmed by a blazing fire on the hearth, and shutting the door on a cold and blustery night? Shelter is what men need in the time of storm.

I will long remember one winter day when I was traveling in China many years ago. The fine rain that began in the morning soon turned to sleet. The narrow footpaths became icy, and I had great difficulty making headway. By nightfall I was chilled to the bone, and still far from my destination. As I came near to a little village I saw an inn, and decided to stop there for the night. I still remember what a sense of peace and security I felt as I sat upon my cot set up in the center of a large room surrounded by friendly fellow travelers. "Let the chill winds blow," I said to myself as I felt the warmth from the burning cornstalks before me on the floor. We were very happy to be *shut in* in this humble place of refuge on that dreary night.

"And the Lord shut him in." These words ring in our ears like a comforting refrain amid the clashing sounds of conflict that echo and re-echo through the world. They remind us that we too may be shut in by the Lord, when the coming storm breaks about our heads as it is sure to do. But there is something we must learn before that storm breaks.

We often speak of certain people as shut-ins. They are those who, because of age or infirmity, find it necessary to be shut away from the world of activity. We sometimes pity them, but how often those who have yielded to such a necessity have developed beautiful characters from whom we may learn lessons of serenity and trust. These may be called "God's shut-ins," for it is God who gives them such peace of mind.

What does it mean to have God shut us in? There are some people who seem to be living in a spiritual shelter. Their home may be a mansion or a basement apartment. That matters not. Afflictions do not seem to lay them low. Annoyances do not upset them. Under all circumstances they are able to maintain a poise that is astonishing to others and a cheerful outlook that is a great blessing to themselves.

Like Job, these people are able to rise above their trials and say, "The Lord gave, and the Lord hath taken away; blessed be the name of the Lord." Satan complained that God had put a hedge about Job. But God demonstrated that that hedge was not material blessings but an inner grace that even the enemy of Job's soul could not touch by his evil darts.

Yes, God does put a hedge about us. But He does it with our cooperation. It was Job's confidence in God and his complete trust that God would always do right that helped him build that hedge.

It is not some modern ark, or a refuge perhaps in the mountains, or a bombproof shelter in the city, in which we are to seek refuge now. It is a serenity of mind that comes from a consciousness that all is well between us and God, and an unflinching faith in God's promises. It is only a spiritual refuge that will keep us safe in the last days.

This is a shelter that must be erected before the storm breaks.

Noah and his family were called to enter the ark seven days before the Flood came. The call to us now is:

"Gather yourselves together, yea, gather together, O nation not desired; before the decree bring forth, before the day pass as the chaff, before the fierce anger of the Lord come upon you, before the day of the Lord's anger come upon you. Seek ye the Lord, all ye meek of the earth, which have wrought his judgment; seek righteousness, seek meekness: it may be ye shall be hid in the day of the Lord's anger." Zephaniah 2:1-3.

What does this experience of entering in include? David tells us in these words:

"Oh how great is thy goodness, which thou hast laid up for them that fear thee; which thou hast wrought for them that trust in thee before the sons of men! Thou shalt hide them in the secret of thy presence from the pride of man: thou shalt keep them secretly in a pavilion from the strife of tongues." Psalm 31:19, 20.

"The pride of man." "The strife of tongues." How often such things as these cause us to lose our Christian composure. How disturbed we often become over something we have seen or heard. In petty trials of daily living we often need a shelter where we can be shut away from things that trouble us. This does not mean that we are to withdraw from the world on such occasions. But it does mean that in the midst of our activity, even when we are face to face with annoying situations, we have a shelter unknown to others to which we may resort, where God can shut us in away from the slights and criticisms, the trials and irritations, that would otherwise destroy our peace.

We need daily to cultivate the habit of seeking such a refuge. Then when great trials come, it will be natural to turn to that refuge rather than seek some human way out of our difficulties and disappointments that may fail us.

The challenge to us now is best described in the words of Jeremiah:

"If thou hast run with the footmen, and they have wearied thee, then how canst thou contend with horses? and if in the land of peace, wherein thou trustedst, they wearied thee, then how wilt thou do in the swelling of Jordan?" Jeremiah 12:5.

When we contend with the footmen of daily trials, let us not grow weary, for in so doing we are fitting ourselves to contend with the horsemen of greater trials. If we become troubled and anxious when life is going along in a comparatively peaceful way, how can we expect to be calm in the flood tide of Jordan?

Too many people are worried about what may happen to them in the days to come. They should be more concerned about finding a spiritual refuge now, for those who have learned lessons of faith and confidence in God now need not fear the future.

So let us enter into this experience. This is what God bids us do. "Come, my people," He says, "enter thou into thy chambers, and shut thy doors about thee: hide thyself as it were for a little moment, until the indignation be overpast." Isaiah 26:20. These words may have an application to the day of the Lord's wrath. They also have a spiritual application for us now.

To build within ourselves such a spiritual shelter should be our daily task. There are four pillars it should have: (1) *Surrender*—which will lead us ever to say, "I am thine, O Lord." "My times are in thy hand." Psalm 31:15. (2) *Resignation*—which helps us to declare, "If God wills it, then it is good." (3) *Obedience*—which causes us to exclaim with Christ, "I delight to do thy will, O my God: yea, thy law is within my heart." Psalm 40:8. (4) *Trust*—which inspires us to proclaim, "In God have I put my trust: I will not be afraid what man can do unto me." Psalm 56:11.

How wonderful it is to know that "the name of the Lord is a strong tower: the righteous runneth into it, and is safe." Proverbs 18:10.

THE RESTING PLACE

"As Noah's dove, sent forth on landward quest,
    O'er the wide Deluge waste, pursued its flight,
And finding near or far no place of rest—
    No spot of earth where longing foot might light—
On wearied wing at length, when day was dead,
Returned unto the haven whence it fled,

"So let my thoughts, when unrestrained within
    By wholesome task, not wander idly forth,
O'er the dark deeps of folly and of sin,
    Where rest is not, nor aught of solid worth,
But turn, as turns the needle toward the pole,
To Christ, the ark and refuge of my soul."

—*Author Unknown*

The Right Way of Escape

WE LIVE in a world of trial and temptation. The issues of life are oftentimes well-nigh overwhelming. Everywhere, there are men and women who are seeking release from some grave difficulty that they cannot surmount, and some hard problem that they cannot solve. Perplexities seem to increase with the passing years. As never before, the world today is full of trouble.

How shall we meet the trials that assail us? Shall it be by summoning a determined stoicism or a fatalistic attitude? Shall we try to find some way to shift responsibilities that are pressing down too hard upon us, or shall we seek to forget our troubles by drowning them in some form of pleasure? There are, indeed, many ways by which man seeks to escape from the realities of an uncertain existence.

One writer has given a vivid picture of this restless seeking for escape on the part of so many today.

"The pressure of modern life, with its hideous and unnatural strains, has filled the world with people who desire to escape from the normal human tasks and responsibilities as they are presented to men in the world of our time. Some suppose that if they could set up housekeeping afresh, they would make less of a mess of it, and they seek divorce. Some take to dope, some to night clubs, some to daily visits to the cinema, some to whisky. Each, according to his temperament and circumstances, tries to find the shortest cut to forgetfulness of real life, because real life is beyond endurance. In ever increasing numbers, men and women throughout the world are seeking what they suppose to be the final escape, in self-destruction.

"For millions of the sons of men, the ordinary task of life has become a thing to be forgotten as often, and for as long, as possible. They are putting themselves to sleep by a variety of methods; it is the only defense they know against the only life they know."

Much is being written these days about "escape psychology," such as is pictured in the preceding paragraphs. Some have gone so far as to suggest that Christianity is just another means of "escape," or as some express it, "a flight from reality." Lenin called religion "the opium of the people."

This is an untrue picture of Christianity. It is not an escape from the responsibilities and realities of life. The true Christian does not shut his eyes to the facts of life. He senses them more keenly than does one whose conscience is dull. He does more than this; he opens his eyes to the reality of God and divine aid.

In His prayer for His disciples Christ did not pray that they be taken from the world, but that they might be kept from its contamination by an inner purity that pervaded the life. The Christian is called the salt of the earth, the light of the world. He is in the world to perform a definite service for mankind.

The Christian can meet life differently from the one who knows not God. He does not seek escape *from* reality but finds escape *in* reality—in the reality of God and His promises. He is able to look at earthly realities unflinchingly because of the greater reality of divine aid.

It was to this that the apostle Paul referred when he wrote to the Corinthian brethren:

"There hath no temptation taken you but such as is common to man: but God is faithful, who will not suffer you to be tempted above that ye are able; but will with the temptation also make a way to escape, that ye may be able to bear it." 1 Corinthians 10:13.

Paul here declares that God makes a way of escape for man when trials overwhelm him, or when strong temptations assail him. This is a true way to find relief from the burdens of life. Said Christ, "Come unto me, all ye that labour and are heavy laden, and I will give you rest." In this sense there is escape in

33

the religion of Christ. But this is far different from the "escape psychology" of which we hear so much.

The Christian faces life, he accepts responsibility, he does not try to run from reality, he does not seek some substitute for life; but he lives the fuller life, he bears the greater burdens, he meets the strong temptations, conscious that the divine hand is upon him as well as upon the fiery trial, and that God will either remove the trial when it becomes too great, or strengthen the whole being to endure it. How much nobler is this attitude than to seek to shirk the severities of life! The "escape" that the world seeks makes of man a weakling. The way of escape to which Paul refers makes a man divinely strong.

This way of escape which God offers to man is not flight but release. A prisoner might escape or flee from prison, but he is a prisoner still; a debtor might successfully avoid his creditor by moving to some distant clime, but he is a debtor still; a sinner might still the compunctions of conscience by an eternal round of pleasure, but he is a sinner still.

Escape, as men usually interpret it, is something that an afflicted person attempts to do for himself. Release is a gift from one of authority. The creditor can release the debtor; a governor can pardon the murderer; God can forgive the sinner. Release is more than escape. It is this that is found in the religion of Christ. Notice the prophetic picture concerning the work of Christ.

"The Spirit of the Lord God is upon me; because the Lord hath anointed me to preach good tidings unto the meek; he hath sent me to bind up the brokenhearted, to proclaim liberty to the captives, and the opening of the prison to them that are bound." Isaiah 61:1.

Again we read, "If the Son therefore shall make you free, ye shall be free indeed." Release from the burden of sin makes one better able to bear the burdens of life. When one is bearing a double burden the load is too heavy. The consciousness of sin saps the vitality and unfits one to meet the issues of life. When the mind and heart are free, burdens seem light, and strong temptations can be met without defeat. This is, no doubt, what Christ meant when He said of Satan, "The prince of this world cometh, and hath nothing in me." Christ's conscience was clear. No sin burdened Him down. He went forth to meet the enemy knowing the righteousness of His heart and cause.

The true Christian is no weakling. He is a tower of strength. He is a stalwart soldier. His strength and assurance are rooted in the verities of God's love and merciful watchcare and in "a conscience void of offence toward God, and toward men." This is the true way of escape, which is offered to all who believe in the Lord Jesus Christ.

Dispelling the Darkness

THE world today presents a dark picture. Wherever one turns there are things which cause distress of heart and mind. Even in that institution, the church, which should be like a light set on a hill, there are shadowy recesses which trouble the heart. The prince of darkness is earnestly at work every day scattering gloom over the whole face of God's creation. He does it by causing men to forget God and to hate their fellow men. He does it by casting doubt upon the very truth of God, and upon those who profess to follow Him. He does it by causing those who bear the light to stumble and fall and extinguish their light.

Unless with a determined heart we turn our faces toward the light, we shall dwell in darkness, for, as the prophet declared, "Darkness shall cover the earth, and gross darkness the people." It is too easy to see the dark side of life. It is too easy to be filled with gloom, for we live amid earth's dark night of sin.

When a man turns from the world and joins the church, he expects to find a different atmosphere—one that is filled with light and rejoicing. Christ has rescued men and women from the darkness and placed their feet on the lighted way. Henceforth they should be living above the shadows and have their faces turned heavenward, where all is light. The trouble is that too many still continue to walk among the shadows or slip off the path into the ways of sin. Thus as one comes into the church and finds that which should not be there, he may be disappointed.

The greatest paradox that one can find in human experience is a man or woman who has found the light of life and still dwells amid the shadows—one who belongs to the church and still finds little there to give him cheer and comfort—for even in the church of God one may find both light and darkness. We may face the light, or we may face the darkness.

Someone has said, "The church is an assembly of imperfect Christians in the process of being made perfect. It is not an assembly of perfect scholars, but a school; not a gallery of completed statues, but an artist's studio where the statues are made; not a showcase of finished goods, but a factory; not a completed building, but one in the process, with the scaffolding and debris still about it."

One must decide for himself what he will look for. If he wishes to find in the church that which will distress him, he may do so. There are failures all about. If he wishes to dwell on the faults of the members, he will find enough to keep his mind occupied every waking moment. If he wishes to spend his time trying to correct the wrongs of others, he will not find sufficient time in the day to cover the list. We have seen people who seem to be possessed with the spirit of faultfinding. One seldom hears a word of commendation or cheer come from their lips. They have many ideas on what ought not to be done, but few on what ought to be done. Their whole attitude is a negative one, and they help to develop such a spirit in the church.

It takes only one or two such souls in a church to keep it in a stir of contention and division all the time, to cast a gloom over the whole church and cause its light to be dimmed.

We admit that there are matters in the church that give us some troubled moments. There are members who are contentious and hard to get along with; there are others who bring disrepute upon the church; there are things that greatly displease us. What are we going to do about it? Think only of these and have our hearts filled with gloom? Or think of the victories that many have had, and of the steady progress that others are making? If you cannot find in the members much to give you cheer, surely you will find it in Christ, whom they profess to serve, and who is patient and merciful and does not easily cast off the sinner.

This good counsel is given to the Christian:

"You will have many perplexities to meet in your Christian life in connection with the church; but do not try too hard to mold your brethren. If you see that they do not meet the requirements of God's word, do not condemn; if they provoke, do not retaliate. When things are said that would exasperate, quietly keep your soul from fretting. You see many things which appear wrong in others, and you want to correct these wrongs. You commence in your own strength to work for a reform; but you do not go about it in the right way. You must labor for the erring with a heart subdued, softened by the Spirit of God, and let the Lord work through you, the agent. Roll your burden on Jesus. You feel that the Lord must take up the case, where Satan is striving for the mastery over some soul; but you are to do what you can in humility and meekness, and put the tangled work, the complicated matters, into the hands of God. Follow the directions in his word, and leave the outcome of the matter to his wisdom. *Having done all you can to save your brother, cease worrying, and go calmly about other pressing duties. It is no longer your matter, but God's.*"—*Testimonies for the Church,* vol. 5, p. 347. (Italics supplied.)

What sound advice! How impatient some are! Many would like to play the part of a surgeon, and that without delay. But the important thing is to save a brother rather than condemn him. Many are the problems that cannot be settled with dispatch; there are matters that only time and God can bring to light. None should, by unsympathetic criticism and harsh condemnation, bring disunity into the church and cause some to forsake God wholly who otherwise might be saved. Again we read concerning this matter:

"Do not, through impatience, cut the knot of difficulty, making matters hopeless. Let God untangle the snarled-up threads for you. He is wise enough to manage the complications of our lives. He has skill and tact. We cannot always see his plans; we must wait patiently their unfolding, and not mar and destroy them. He will reveal them to us in his own good time. Seek for unity; cultivate love and conformity to Christ in all things."—*Ibid.,* p. 348.

The biggest problem that anyone should find in the church is with himself. If God can keep us humble when others are proud and boastful, patient when others threaten, hopeful when others doubt, cheerful when others are spreading gloom, helpful to those who stray, then we shall fulfill our lot in the church of God and be a blessing to many.

We are reminded of a story related by J. R. Miller in his little book *Glimpses Through Life's Windows.* He writes:

"In a sick-room there was a little rose-bush in a pot in the window. There was only one rose on the bush, and its face was turned full toward the light. This fact was noticed and spoken of, when one said that the rose would look no other way save toward the light. Experiments had been made with it; it had been turned away from the window, its face toward the gloom of the interior, but in a little time it would resume its old position. With wonderful persistence it refused to keep its face toward the darkness and insisted on ever looking toward the light."

Dear reader, when you are tempted to dwell upon the failures of others, remember the potted rose. Keep your face turned toward the light and shun the darkness. I repeat the words previously quoted: "Having done all you can to save your brother, cease worrying, and go calmly about other pressing duties. It is no longer your matter, but God's."

OUR DISCONTENT

"Ah, how Christ's patience shames our discontent!
How foolish all our fretfulness appears!
Did he not love us all these weary years?
And yet his days in quiet toil were spent.
He knew the cause whereunto he was sent:
His world stood waiting, there were anguished tears
For him to wipe, the dead upon their biers
To be awaked, and men called to repent,
And little children to be blessed, the hill
Of Calvary to climb; yet day by day
Unrecognized, he calmly worked until
The time was come. O blessed Lord, we pray
That by thy life we may take pattern still,
And in thy path may follow patiently."

—*Selected*

39

What Shall We Do With Worry?

"THERE are many whose hearts are aching under a load of care because they seek to reach the world's standard. They have chosen its service, accepted its perplexities, adopted its customs. Thus their character is marred, and their life made a weariness. The continual worry is wearing out the life forces. . . . Worry is blind, and can not discern the future; but Jesus sees the end from the beginning. In every difficulty He has His way prepared to bring relief."—*The Desire of Ages,* p. 330.

Let us ponder these words carefully when we are inclined to worry. They are in harmony with Christ's direct command: "Be not anxious for your life, what ye shall eat, or what ye shall drink; nor yet for your body, what ye shall put on." Matthew 6:25, A.R.V. To be overanxious is to worry. Christ commands us to stop it. He gives several reasons for doing so. He is speaking to one who acknowledges God as his Maker and Lord.

First, worry over material things does not concern itself with that which is most important. Christ emphasizes this when He says, "Is not the life more than meat, and the body than raiment?" On another occasion He said, "Man shall not live by bread alone" (Matthew 4:4); and again, "A man's life consisteth not in the abundance of the things which he possesseth." Luke 12:15. There is within us a higher spiritual nature that is not dependent on temporal circumstances. One can live in poverty and still have peace with God. He can be imprisoned and still feel more of the spirit of true freedom than those entangled with the cares of life.

Second, worry is a reflection on God. It reveals a lack of faith in God. It doubts that God knows what is needed, or if He does, that He cares. This is something that no child of God dare consciously admit. Christ calls this to our attention as He refers to God's sustaining mercies over the birds and the flowers. Are we of less value than they? He asks. Thus He argues His point with us, and then adds, "Your Father knoweth that ye have need of these things." Verse 30. Surely this is enough to silence us, and cause us to lay aside our useless worries.

Third, Christ makes it plain that worry is foolish. "Which of you," said He, "by being anxious can add one cubit unto the measure of his life?" Matthew 6:27, A.R.V.

This is why we are told that worry is blind and unreasonable. We worry because we feel like it, and for no other reason. But feeling is an inconsistent emotion that should never be allowed to dominate us. One who permits himself to be buffeted about by the whims and fancies of his feelings is like a ship without a rudder. He will find himself at cross-purposes with the current of life about him, or will be driven whither he would not go.

Worry should be shunned like the plague. It is dangerous. Emotional upset brought about by worry may be the cause of much physical harm. Few have looked upon worry in such a light, and too many have thought that it is something in which they can freely indulge without great harm. Indeed, it is strange that there seems to be some perverse satisfaction in such self-afflicted pain as is caused by worry. But how foolish and useless to add torture to one's daily trials.

Worry merely adds to the load of life's burdens we have to carry. It does not attempt to lighten the load. If it did, then there might be some little value in it. Worry is not concentrated thought. It is just doing nothing. One does not worry when actively engaged in mastering difficulties. When the mind is properly employed, fear seldom finds entrance. It is when one has some time on his hands, and has opportunity for reflection, that he has to contend with this evil.

You say, "Yes, I know it is useless to worry, but I just can't help it." But you can do something to help it. Here is one good suggestion that is given to us by Roy L. Smith, well-known editor and author:

41

"When we find ourselves worrying, we must begin praying aggressively, not pleading with God for deliverance from our fears, but calmly and positively asserting our faith in God as *one who has always delivered us*. To beg and implore God for help only increases the strain, excites the little gland [that is affected by our emotions], and makes tense the whole system. To declare our confidence, to reassure ourselves of God's loving care, and to insist upon the fact of his solicitude on our behalf is to quiet the nerves, restore the little gland to normalcy, and to find life developing calm and poise."

Another way you can help it is to beware of not occupying your leisure moments. Seek out some unselfish employment. Visit someone not so fortunate as you are, and pass on a cheery word of comfort. Or sit down and write a good letter to some friend or relative, avoiding all reference to unpleasant things. Doing anything that will substitute thoughts concerning the welfare of someone else for thoughts of self will have a most beneficial effect.

Discipline is another thing you can do to help keep you from worry. Discipline is a hard taskmaster, you say? But it is not half so hard a taskmaster as worry, and its rewards are peace and rest. Yes, we must take hold of ourselves and say, "Worry, be gone. I will give you room no longer. You have taken altogether too much of my attention." Turn it out of your house and let it sit on your doorstep if it will. But have nothing more to do with it. You will be surprised at the results. More often than not your worry will scamper away when it finds itself left out in the cold, and will never come back again. Of course, being the creatures that we are, other feelings of the same stripe will seek entrance into our minds; but with a strict purpose to permit no thoughts of fear and apprehension to linger long on your premises, you will be going a long way to conquer worry.

We are told that worry is what continues after a danger is past or before it arrives, and that it thrives on pure imagination. If it is this kind of worry that troubles you, it should be treated with disciplined action. If it is caused by some real problem—like the payment of a debt, making a wrong right, doing a certain piece of work that you fear is beyond your ability to do as well as may be expected, or just performing the daily duties that for one reason or another have come to loom too large for you to cope with—then sit down in a serious but not a morbid mood, and face the issue. Do the best you can to solve the problem. Pray for a right spirit. Do not let personal gain or loss affect your decision one way or another. Be surrendered to God's will whatever the trial may be. He will help you even more certainly than your closest friend. If after you have done all this, you still cannot see the light, do nothing more about it for the present, and dismiss it wholly from your mind.

No great harm can come to you from such a course. If some blow must come because of your failure to solve your problem, then take the blow in good grace. You will most certainly find that it will not be half so hard as you anticipated. And there may be a surprising turn of events that will remind you how foolish you were to harbor worry even for a few moments.

Someone may advise you to run around the block to help overcome your fears. But, says Norman Vincent Peale, noted New York City pastor, not everybody can do that. "If you ran around the block here in New York, in all probability the policeman would take after you." This he says to emphasize a surer plan than mere human remedies to bring you peace of mind. "The one sure method of eradicating fear from the human mind is by surrendering one's life to God," he more solemnly declares. And to this we add, Let there be complete obedience to His will, as it is revealed from day to day, for, say the Scriptures, "Great peace have they which love thy law: and nothing shall offend them." Psalm 119:165.

Today Is Not Too Long

CHRIST was a wise counselor. He was the forerunner of all those writers, pastors, and physicians who attempt to help the mentally ill. He laid down principles upon which much of the advice given today is built. No word of His to the overanxious is more helpful than the admonition: "Take therefore no thought for the morrow: for the morrow shall take thought for the things of itself. Sufficient unto the day is the evil thereof." Matthew 6:34.

Some fifty years ago the celebrated physician Sir William Osler gave a lecture to the students of Yale University on the mental attitude toward perplexing problems. He told them that they should form "the habit of a life of Day-Tight Compartments." "The future is today," he said; "there is no tomorrow." This thought is being emphasized in popular works on peace of mind today. There is a sound principle in it that helps to relieve anxiety.

Divide your duties into portions no longer than one day, and you will at once find your mountains laid low. Attack the job at hand. Do your best each day, and, lo, the great task you feared is done. Go to the ant, and watch him pick up his little grain of sand and move on. You see him today, and again tomorrow, working away steadily until his job is done. The faith that removes mountains is the faith that keeps us going on hopefully, making the most of each day though appearances may be against us.

God was good when He began life in this world on a day-by-

44

day basis. He might have done this mighty work in one majestic stroke. He might have made one long day as years to divide the life of man. But He set the world to rotating about the sun at a pace that would meet human needs. Just twenty-four hours of time marks off our days, and we can say to ourselves, "I failed yesterday, but I have another day to meet my trials with better grace."

Christ taught His disciples to pray, "Give us this day our daily bread." If we be fed today, and every day, what more can we ask? Of old, the Lord promised His people, "As thy days, so shall thy strength be." Deuteronomy 33:25. And thus we sing:

> "Lord, for tomorrow and its needs I do not pray;
>   Keep me, my God, from stain of sin
> Just for today.
> Help me to labor earnestly, and duly pray;
>   Let me be kind in word and deed,
> Father, today."

As we go forth each morning, let us say to ourselves, "Today is not too long. In its brief hours I can do right, master the passions that seek the rule over me, meet the trials that cause me to fear, and surmount the problems that present themselves. God has promised to give me strength for today. I will keep that promise in mind and claim it until the night calls me back to slumber."

That is the only way we can press on to the high goal that is set before us and not faint. Refuse to consider those fearful promptings about tomorrow. Tell your good self that you will face all the fears of the future when tomorrow comes. You have courage and strength sufficient to go through the day, but not so if you add to today's burdens the problems and trials that you may expect tomorrow.

"We are to follow Christ day by day. God does not bestow help for to-morrow. He does not give His children all the directions for their life journey at once, lest they should become confused. He tells them just as much as they can remember and perform. The strength and wisdom imparted are for the present emergency. 'If any of you lack wisdom,'—for to-day,—'let him ask of God, that giveth to all men liberally, and upbraideth not; and it shall be given him.' "—*The Desire of Ages,* p. 313.

"The habit of brooding over anticipated evils is unwise and unchristian. In thus doing, we fail to enjoy the blessings and to improve the opportunities of the present. The Lord requires us to perform the duties of to-day, and to endure its trials. We are to-day to watch that we offend not in word or deed. We must to-day praise and honor God. By the exercise of living faith to-day, we are to conquer the enemy."—*Testimonies for the Church,* vol. 5, p. 200.

It is a comfort to be able to say to God, as did the psalmist, "My times are in thy hand," and then leave the mysterious, uncertain future with Him.

When we weigh out our problems in portions for one day, the burdens do not seem so heavy. More often it is the future that haunts us, and not the present. In the moment of challenge we seem to be able to summon sufficient strength to meet the trial. And those who have not burdened their minds about the cares of some coming day are better able to meet the issues of today.

We must ever remember, too, that it is largely the way we relate ourselves to the happenings of each day that determines the size of our problems. If, as one has advised, we "bear lightly the things that needs must be," then very possibly we have more than halved our burden. If we kick against the pricks, wrangle within our souls over slights and mistreatment, fret because we are not free to do as we please, we make the obstacles before us almost insurmountable. How wonderful it is that God has given us a mind that can so adapt itself to circumstances as almost to create a new world in which to live. It is not so much the burden, but what we think about the burden, that weighs us down.

Reinhold Niebuhr puts this prayer on our lips:

"God grant me the serenity
  To accept the things I cannot change;
  The courage to change the things I can;
  And the wisdom to know the difference."

Martin Luther once well said, "I know from my own experience as well as from that of all troubled souls, that it is solely our own self-conceit which is at the root of all our disquietude."

How easy it is for human beings to feel that life has not meted out to them what their talents or their labors deserve.

Others may have trials and conflicts, be afflicted by sickness or want, be thrust aside for someone else; but when it happens to us, that is too much to bear, and we go about nursing our wounds and adding to the load that others must carry along the road through life.

How much better it would be to take a different attitude from that. A change in our outlook could make all the difference between sullen defeat and joyous triumph over circumstances.

Then there are those loads of grievance too many bear. Someone has spoken unkindly, has uttered words of criticism, has even insulted us. How we would like to give back in kind, but we have restrained ourselves, though we have not unburdened ourselves of the bitterness. The Bible wisely admonishes all such, "Let not the sun go down upon your wrath." Ephesians 4:26.

Yes, the slights and wrongs are sufficient unto the day. It does not pay to carry them over to another day. If misunderstandings have arisen, each night before we go to rest let us say to ourselves, "Yes, I was hurt today, but I'll forget it. What difference does it make in the long run? Maybe it was the fruit of my own doings. In that case I'll make amends."

Better still, do not let a day go by before straightening out some misunderstanding, if at all possible, by sincere explanation or humble apology. Why carry that load over to another day?

Let us go forth each new day with fresh courage and seek to do our best in the strength that God portions out to us.

THE DAY'S NEEDS

"Each day I pray, God give me strength anew,
To do the task I do not wish to do;
To yield obedience, not asking why;
To love and own the truth and scorn to lie;
To look a cold world bravely in the face;
To cheer for those that pass me in the race;
To bear my burdens gaily, unafraid;
To lend a hand to those that need my aid;
To measure what I am by what I give;
God, give me strength that I may rightly live!"
—*British Weekly*

47

Are You a Slave
to Feelings?

AS YOU walk somewhat sprightly down the street on your way to work, you meet a friend. In answer to your salutation, "How are you this morning?" he replies, "I don't feel so well."

"So you don't feel well. Just what is the matter? Does your head ache?" you ask.

"No," he replies.

"Does your back ache?"

"No."

"Are you ill?"

"No. I just feel miserable."

There is not much more to say to that except, "Too bad." And then you part. Your friend goes on with dejected mien, and you continue your way, pondering on the subject of feelings.

What makes us feel the way we do sometimes? We cannot point to any definite cause. Bad feelings, good feelings—they seem to come and go without rhyme or reason. Buoyed up by good feelings, or dejected by bad feelings, we go forth to meet the world. Of course, in accordance with proper behavior, we do not, child-like, let our feelings run riot, slapping this one and that one on the back when we feel good, and slapping them otherwise when the mood has changed to a dark, impatient one.

Solomon said, "He that ruleth his spirit" is better "than he that taketh a city." Proverbs 16:32. And he warns that "he that hath no rule over his own spirit is like a city that is broken down, and without walls." Proverbs 25:28.

How shall we rule our spirits? When we are unhappy shall it be by a keep-down-there-I-do-not-want-anyone-to-see-you attitude? Although this way of doing may be heroic, it may be harmful not only to the soul but to the body as well.

Suppression is not a good way to deal with bad feelings. Substitution is the better course to take. Rid yourself of them by substituting encouraging thoughts concerning God, special interests that will hold your attention, consideration for others who may be in need. Do not close your door upon the problems, the disappointments, the misunderstandings that have disturbed you, and keep them shut up inside. Open your mind's door wide, bid them be gone, and invite pleasant thoughts to take their place.

A person's bad feelings as far as the mental state is concerned may be due directly to ill-health. That is something which may require the attention of a physician. But many times our miserable feelings have sprung from some action over which we have control, such as resentment because of some unjust act, bitterness because of misunderstanding or misrepresentation, weariness because of boredom with our lot, distrust and envy for one reason or another. Any number of emotions may be the root of misery.

In such instances we must substitute tolerance for resentment, kindness for bitterness, interest in the place of lassitude, confidence in the place of distrust, and sympathy in the place of envy. For every bad emotion there is an antidote.

Christ recognized this helpful factor in the life when He said, "But I say unto you, Love your enemies, bless them that curse you, do good to them that hate you, and pray for them which despitefully use you, and persecute you." Matthew 5:44.

Two people may be having the same trying experience, but one meets the challenge and says, "I will not allow unpleasant thoughts to possess me. I will trust God and be happy." The other, like Jacob, cries out in the misery of his soul, "All these things are against me," thus adding to his burdens.

> "Two men toiled side by side from sun to sun,
>   And both were poor;
>   Both sat with children, when the day was done,
>   About the door.

49

"One saw the beautiful crimson cloud
    And shining moon;
The other with his head in sadness bowed,
    Made night of noon.

"One loved each tree and flower and singing bird
    On mount or plain:
No music in the soul of one was stirred
    By leaf or rain.

"One saw the good in every fellow man,
    And hoped the best;
The other marveled at his Master's plan,
    And doubt confessed.

"One having God above and heaven below,
    Was satisfied;
The other, discontented, lived in woe,
    And hopeless died."
                    —London *S.S. Times*

Paul gave us good counsel when he said, "Follow after the things which make for peace." Romans 14:19. Some people invite ill feelings by their attitudes toward those about them. Some are pugnacious, and others are easily offended. Still others are unbending and find it hard to yield to persuasion. It is little wonder that such persons find life difficult. Why not seek to avoid sharp clashes of opinion, or situations that may give offense? Why not have a teachable spirit at all times? This is no doubt the way to follow after the things that make for peace.

On another occasion the great apostle gave helpful instruction along this line when he wrote to the Philippians:

"Finally, brethren, whatsoever things are true, whatsoever things are honest, whatsoever things are just, whatsoever things are pure, whatsoever things are lovely, whatsoever things are of good report; if there be any virtue, and if there be any praise, think on these things." Philippians 4:8.

How much distress, ill will, and weariness we might avoid by such an attitude of mind! It is in the mind that most of our miserable feelings originate. The will is the guardian of the mind, and it should continually be brought into use to control the thoughts. This is a God-given power that aids us in choosing the right and rejecting the evil. To all those who choose to think right thoughts, and find it difficult to do so, Christ says, "My grace is sufficient for thee: for my strength is made perfect in weakness." 2 Corinthians 12:9.

At times, no matter what we may or may not do, unhappy feelings will arise within us. We do not know why this is so. But this should not discourage us. Our knowledge of acceptance with God is not to be based on feelings. Very often the most devout person has to contend with the forces of darkness.

"Many make a serious mistake in their religious life by keeping the attention fixed upon their feelings, and thus judging of their advancement or decline. Feelings are not a safe criterion. We are not to look within for evidence of our acceptance with God. We shall find there nothing but that which will discourage us. Our only hope is in 'looking unto Jesus, who is. the author and finisher of our faith.' There is everything in him to inspire with hope, with faith, and with courage. He is our righteousness, our consolation and rejoicing."—*Testimonies for the Church,* vol. 5, p. 199.

"Feelings are often deceiving, emotions are no sure safeguard; for they are variable and subject to external circumstances. Many are deluded by relying on sensational impressions. The test is, What are you *doing* for Christ? What sacrifices are you making? What victories are you gaining? A selfish spirit overcome, a temptation to neglect duty resisted, passion subdued, and willing, cheerful obedience rendered to the will of Christ, is far greater evidence that you are a child of God than spasmodic piety and emotional religion."—*Ibid.,* vol. 4, p. 188.

Let us learn to rule the spirit and not be swayed by our feelings, whether they be good or ill. Calm confidence in a loving heavenly Father, faith sufficient for the day, and absorbing interest in duties that beckon—these are marvelous aids to constancy and happiness under any circumstance.

The Dark Shadow of Discouragement

THE world is filled with disillusioned and troubled souls. Frustration, indignation, and despair lead many to cry out, "Woe is me!" as did the prophet Micah long ago. Who has not felt the chill of blasted hopes, rank injustice, and cold ingratitude! The dark shadow of discouragement haunts the lives of millions today.

How shall we meet this challenge to our peace of mind? The ancient prophet, who at one time met with much to distress him, records his answer to this question in the seventh chapter of his book.

"Woe is me!" he writes, "for I am as when they have gathered the summer fruits, as the grapegleanings of the vintage: there is no cluster to eat: my soul desired the firstripe fruit." Here is pictured great disappointment. Desiring fruit and rightly expecting it in the time of harvest, Micah finds the vines empty. It was like the experience of Christ, who being hungered, approached a fig tree and found no figs. How often we too meet with such frustrating situations in life.

Then the prophet laments, "The good man is perished out of the earth: and there is none upright among men. . . . The best of them is as a brier: the most upright is sharper than a thorn hedge." Here is portrayed bitter disappointment and indignation. The seer had expected much of men, but they had often failed him. Even the best seemed to do hurtful things, and he felt like the psalmist, who confessed, "I said in my haste, All men are liars." Psalm

116:11. Yes, human frailty is evident on every hand, often causing righteous indignation to rise within us even today.

But there was something that troubled Micah more than this. "Trust ye not in a friend," wrote the despairing prophet, "put ye not confidence in a guide. . . . A man's enemies are the men of his own house." Those dearest to him proved faithless. This was the climax to his trials, the last straw, as we say today. No wonder he was led to cry out, "Woe is me!" We may endure the blow of hopes deferred, the sting of unjust dealings; but the bad faith of those from whom we expected much often is more than we can bear.

But what should we do about this? What a pity if anyone should cause us to lose our way to the kingdom! What did Micah do? After relating these disheartening experiences which brought him so much inner conflict, he exclaimed:

"Therefore I will look unto the Lord; I will wait for the God of my salvation: my God will hear me. Rejoice not against me, O mine enemy: when I fall, I shall arise; when I sit in darkness, the Lord shall be a light unto me. . . . He will bring me forth to the light, and I shall behold his righteousness."

Fully recognizing that the situation about him was not encouraging, he deliberately turned and looked in another direction. There seemed to be little on earth to give him hope: even friends proved untrue, and those who should have been children of light walked in darkness. No wonder discouragement overtook him. But he refused to be held in its clutches. He admitted that he had fallen into a gloomy mood, but he determined that he would face the light shining from the Sun of Righteousness.

"When I fall, I shall arise; when I sit in darkness, the Lord shall be a light unto me." Here is a sure remedy for discouragement. Here is a golden motto that every Christian should hang on memory's walls. We should refuse to sit in darkness and nurse our wounds. There are light and healing for the disheartened. Darkness may cover the earth and gross darkness the people, but, says the prophet Isaiah, "The Lord shall arise upon thee [as a light], and his glory shall be seen upon thee." None need brood in some chilling cavern. The call of Heaven is, "Come forth into the light, and behold the righteousness of the Lord."

Pity the man or woman who, forgetting the faithfulness of

God, feeds on the husks of other men's failures. Surely there is enough in the world, and even in the church, where the wheat and the tares dwell together until the harvest, to breed discouragement and despair. But remember, the Lord too is in the church, and He is pure and righteous. And furthermore, He has imbued many of His dear followers with His same spirit and life. Why not refuse to look upon that which brings gloom into the life, and turn to the One who never fails and to those who with honest hearts endeavor to walk in His ways!

You may take your choice. Feed on the husks, as did the prodigal son in the first stage of his experience; or you may say, as did this same lad when his soul was truly awakened to the beauty and wonder of his father's household, "I will arise and go to my father." Let us rise and leave the seat of the scornful and take a place among the devout, who are looking unto Jesus, the Author and Finisher of our faith.

This may not be so easy to do as it is to mention, but it is the only way to conquer discouragement. Perplexity and bewilderment come at times to most of us for one reason or another. We see and hear things that cause apprehension and even indignation. But we must learn to face these things as did the victorious men of old.

Paul met all this. Among the list of trials that afflicted the apostle, he mentioned "perils among false brethren" (2 Corinthians 11:26) and "the care of all the churches" (verse 28). To the youthful Timothy he wrote of some who had erred from the truth and who had sought to overthrow the faith of the believers. Then he dismissed it all abruptly by declaring, "Nevertheless the foundation of God standeth sure, having this seal, The Lord knoweth them that are his. And, Let every one that nameth the name of Christ depart from iniquity." 2 Timothy 2:19.

The Christian's first concern should be that he is right with God. Once he is assured that he is a child of God, he may properly ignore every circumstance and say, as did Paul, "Nevertheless." This is the watchword of saints. It should often be upon our lips. Facing the problems of life, the Christian is to keep his faith and cry, "Nevertheless." The times may be evil. All that life holds dear may seem uncertain. Men may disappoint us; friends may come and go; but the foundation of God's church standeth sure! Here is something that never fails. No cloud ever shadows its glory. No taint ever tarnishes its purity. What we need to do is to become more definitely a part of it, and to understand it better.

At the most distressing period in David's experience, when his popularity had waned for the time being, when almost everyone was turning against him, and all seemed confusion among God's people, the Scripture says of him, "David was greatly distressed; for the people spake of stoning him, because the soul of all the people was grieved, . . . *but David encouraged himself in the Lord his God.*" 1 Samuel 30:6.

This is a blessed retreat for the discouraged. There are always light and hope where God dwells. In moments of disappointment, when we are tempted to doubt and feel greatly troubled, let us turn quickly to Him who loves us with an everlasting love. At the feet of Jesus we lay our burdens down. He bids us, "Come unto me, all ye that labour and are heavy laden, and I will give you rest." Matthew 11:28.

Micah, Paul, and David learned under bitter circumstances the secret of confidence and peace in a faithless and uncertain world. If we would be victors at last, we too must learn this lesson well. It is best expressed in these inspired words of Micah:

"When I fall, I shall arise; when I sit in darkness, the Lord shall be a light unto me." Micah 7-8.

How Jesus Met Life's Problems

LISTEN to Jesus as He tells the perplexed, confused, and nervous Mr. and Mrs. Jones of His day, who want to be sure they have the wherewithal to provide themselves with the best life has to offer:

"Lay not up for yourselves treasures upon earth."

"Take no thought for your life, what ye shall eat, or what ye shall drink; nor yet for your body, what ye shall put on."

"No man can serve two masters. . . . Ye cannot serve God and mammon."

This is all very perplexing to the worldly-minded. Strange doctrine this! What! Not give attention to physical needs and comforts! How can this be? Bills must be paid. The body must be clothed. Food must be provided. We must have a shelter too. Is Christ sanctioning indifference to one's responsibilities? Is He encouraging pauperism?

No! He is merely trying to simplify life for Mr. and Mrs. Jones by telling them to stop a moment in their feverish rush, and think of God.

Behold, He says, how a loving Father cares for the birds. Take note how He clothes the flowers. "Are ye not much better than they?" Do this, He adds, "Seek ye first the kingdom of God, and his righteousness; and all these things shall be added unto you." No, not the luxuries, but your heavenly Father knows what you have need of.

It is wonderful how a calm trust in God can help to simplify life. But what about those bills? Mrs. Jones wants to know.

For one thing, the man or woman who seeks first the kingdom of heaven and its righteousness will not have so many bills to worry about. But to pay the legitimate obligations, we must work and labor with a will. Christ had no use for the indolent man, for one who does not give men their due.

Remember how Jesus rebuked the man of one talent for his waste and indifference? Then think of what He said when Peter told Him about the tribute money. He could have refused to pay this Temple tax on the basis of His priesthood; yet because the leaders did not recognize Him as a priest, He said:

"Notwithstanding, lest we should offend them, go thou to the sea, and cast an hook, and take up the fish that first cometh up; and when thou hast opened his mouth, thou shalt find a piece of money: that take, and give unto them for me and thee." Matthew 17:27.

If Jesus could direct Peter to a fish with a coin in its mouth, could He not have stooped down to the earth where He was standing and picked up the coin? But that would have been too easy. Peter had to work for that coin, even though a miracle was performed in his behalf. No one knows how much time Peter put in before he caught that fish. No, Jesus even in His simplicity toward life did not countenance slothfulness.

What was Christ's attitude toward the natural dangers that arise from time to time? This is best illustrated in the experience of Jesus on the stormy Galilee, as related in Mark 4:35-41. After a day of labor Jesus and His disciples took ship to pass over the lake on the other side. "And there arose a great storm of wind, and the waves beat into the ship, so that it was now full. And he was in the hinder part of the ship, asleep on a pillow: and they awake him, and say unto him, Master, carest thou not that we perish?"

How confused the disciples were! How complicated their task! The winds were blowing; the rain, perhaps, was beating upon them; the waves were dashing into the boat. We can well imagine how busy they were, trying to save themselves, first rowing in this direction and that, then tending the sail, or bailing out the water. In their very cry to the Master they revealed the tension they were under.

After rebuking the winds and calming the sea He had a lesson to give to those disciples. "How is it that ye have no faith?" All their confusion of mind and heart was met with just one word—*faith!* How simple the answer. Does this really help even in times of danger? "Try it!" That is Christ's word to us. Happy are those who have learned the lesson faith.

But there were other matters that Christ would not permit to complicate His life. The personal threats against His life, for instance, and His knowledge that someday those threats would be fulfilled. How did He meet them? Again it was the simplicity of Jesus that helped Him to conquer.

On one occasion the Pharisees sought to frighten Him, saying, "Get thee out, and depart hence: for Herod will kill thee." Luke 13:31.

To this Jesus replied, "Go and tell that fox, 'Behold, I cast out demons and perform cures today and tomorrow, and the third day I finish my course. Nevertheless I must go on my way today and tomorrow and the day following.' " Luke 13:32, 33, R.S.V.

Jesus would permit nothing to complicate His life, not even the hostility of a king. He had a life plan, and followed it calmly. He would not be diverted from the purpose God had laid out for Him. "I must go on my way today and tomorrow and the day following."

How simple that course. Why make life hard by worrying over what a Herod may do day after tomorrow? How was it that Jesus could face the trials and dangers with such poise? It was because He had an unwavering belief that no one could hinder Him until that work was finished. Again and again He would say that His "hour was not yet come."

Concerning His work He declared:

"For I came down from heaven, not to do mine own will, but the will of him that sent me." John 6:38. "My meat is to do the will of him that sent me, and to finish his work." John 4:34. "As my Father hath taught me, I speak these things." John 8:28. "The Son can do nothing of himself, but what he seeth the Father do." John 5:19. "The Father that dwelleth in me, he doeth the works." John 14:10.

The consciousness that God was directing Him to a great and important goal is what kept Jesus at His task even when the day was dark and threatening. Every morning He must have said to

Himself, "I must go on my way today and tomorrow and the day following."

And we can see Him trudging along that dusty road as we read the gospel story. On and on He went. One day as He was about to go into Judea to see Lazarus, who was ill unto death, His disciples protested, "Master, the Jews of late sought to stone thee; and goest thou thither again?" John 11:8.

"Jesus answered, Are there not twelve hours in the day? If any man walk in the day, he stumbleth not, because he seeth the light of this world." Verse 9. By this He meant that as long as a man is walking in the light of God's appointment he has nothing to fear.

But one day those threats caught up with Him. He had brushed them aside many times in the past months, but now He knew His time had come. Still on He went—into the Garden to pray, into the judgment hall to hear men revile and condemn Him, and on out through the gate to Calvary, bearing His cross.

Was this to be the end of a life of such simple trust and faith? Would not God intervene to deliver? Would Jesus not perform some miracle to escape? So thought the disciples. No, this was the way He must go for the present. He knew there could be no turning. Surely the time would come when such simplicity and steadfastness would be vindicated.

And indeed it did! Behold Him rising triumphant over the tomb and all the vicissitudes of life!

The only way you, dear reader, can keep life from becoming complicated and confused is to emulate the simplicity of Jesus. Believe in your soul that God has a dominant purpose for you and that He will direct your footsteps as long as you are obedient to His will. Do not permit the cares of life to entangle you, but go on your way today and tomorrow and the day after with the calm assurance that you are following Jesus and will finally share in His glorious triumph.

Beside Still Waters

HENRY DRUMMOND once wrote, "What sweet delight a quiet life affords." But that was before the automobile and the radio. The bustle and noise of these modern times give little place for quietude. The dominant note today is one of restless activity. A pause in the day's labor seems so much time lost. An hour's wait for some appointment causes one to fidget and grow impatient. Few have learned how to use with profit a period of leisure.

Because of this the world is full of men who have acquired much of material things but lack the capacity to enjoy life on its highest level. The pursuit of earthly gain to the exclusion of character building is total loss, no matter how large the hoard of stocks and bonds. That is why so many rich are often unhappy, and so many poor are ready to sing, "Praise God from whom all blessings flow."

We must renew the delight of a quiet life if we would attain to the stature of Christian manhood and womanhood that God purposes for us. "Meditation is the life of the soul." "The heart that is to be filled to the brim with holy joy must be held still." These words from men of great experience in earlier years contain much wisdom. They have proved true again and again. Life cannot broaden and deepen where the throng gathers for fun or barter. Only as one withdraws for a time to a quiet spot where undisturbed he can let his thoughts roam in higher spheres than that of money and things can he find true satisfaction.

The psalmist said of the Good Shepherd, "He leadeth me beside the still waters." Yes, He goes before us, and if we follow on, He will lead us to quiet resting places, and there speak to us of eternal joys.

Will we let Him lead us? is the great question. Do we love the pleasure-bent crowd? Are we enamored with the quest for worldly gain? Are we busy with many things except the one thing needful? Are we letting the Saviour pass on before us while we remain behind in the heedless throng?

The psalmist cries out, "O taste and see that the Lord is good." Only those who have experienced the joy of meditation beside still waters far from the noise of city and highway know what the sweet singer of Israel is talking about. There amid nature in its untarnished beauty, with only the songbirds to break the silence, our minds most naturally ascend to God. And as we contemplate His majesty and His goodness we find sweet peace that passes all understanding.

What a pity that we cannot find more opportunities for such an experience. Nevertheless let us not excuse ourselves because of this. But let us determine to find some spot somewhere each day to be alone with God. In the retreat of a room, morning, noon, or night, in a secluded spot in a city park, out in the country beside a little-used road, let us seek the "still waters" beside which our Shepherd desires to lead us. Only thus can we know the fullness of holy joy, or find the satisfaction of sweet content from which we may draw the strength and poise that are so necessary to the victorious Christian in these restless times.

In our continual preoccupation with earthly matters do we give God a chance to speak to us? How He longs to give us a word of comfort or courage, but finds us so busy with the affairs of life that He is unable to attract our attention.

I picked up the phone and dialed a certain number. The busy signal sounded. I waited awhile and dialed again. But still the person I wished to speak to was engaged in conversation with someone else. After some time I once more lifted the phone and tried to get through, but that continuous hum still blocked me. What chance had I to deliver an important bit of news that would have made the person very happy?

Imagine, if you can, a king passing a humble dwelling every

day, wishing to bestow upon the inmates some portion of his bounty. But either he finds the place locked against him while the tenants are away on various errands or else he finds them so occupied with home cares that his knock is unheard. So even while the king seeks opportunity to do them good the occupants of this abode may be complaining at their hard lot or feeling greatly troubled because the king seems to care nought for them.

Deep in the mountain country of Sinai, God taught Elijah a very important lesson. The prophet was weak and discouraged, and as he threw himself down inside a cave far from the haunts of men he cried, "I, even I only, am left; and they seek my life."

Elijah had been very zealous for the Lord. He had gone from place to place warning the people against apostasy. He hailed the evil prophets of Baal before him, and challenged them to a test of power. What crowded days those were! Early and late he fought the battles of the Lord.

Then came that mighty hour when before Israel and the frenzied representatives of Baal he called down fire from heaven to demonstrate the power of the God of Abraham, Isaac, and Jacob. Then followed the terrible retribution that fell upon the Baalites, in which Elijah played a major part. The prophet had no doubt sapped much of his vitality and nervous energy to bring about this work of reformation. He was wholly undone and unprepared to meet the storm that was about to break over his own head. Had he failed to give God a chance to refresh his soul?

Now as he sits alone, wondering about his experience, God calls him forth to stand at the entrance of the cave. There He gives the prophet a greatly needed object lesson. First a strong wind shook the mountains and broke in pieces the rocks. Then followed a great earthquake, and after this a consuming fire. These mighty demonstrations were typical of Elijah's life thus far. He had thundered against sin and called down fire from heaven. But that was not enough. He lacked a calm and meditative spirit. After these manifestations of divine majesty had subsided and all nature lay quiet before him, this distraught man of God heard in the silence a still small voice speaking to his heart.

Let us give God a chance to replenish our depleted spiritual strength as in silence we turn aside from the activities of life and listen for the "still small voice."

Christ does not call upon us to withdraw from society, and live unto ourselves, like some recluse in the desert seeking to acquire virtue by his isolation and hardship, but He does bid us, "Come ye yourselves apart into a desert place, and rest a while." When He prayed for His disciples He asked not that God would remove them from the world but that He would keep them from its evil. They were to be a leaven among men, a light to the world. They must keep in constant contact with life, and influence its course. But how could they be sure that the leaven would not lose its effectiveness and that the light would not grow dim? Some attention must be given to that. Fresh leaven must be added to the lump. And the lamp must be trimmed and replenished with oil.

This is why He bids us come apart to some quiet retreat. The time may be brief in comparison to the long periods for work that must be done. But that little while—how essential it is! We cannot through ceaseless toil accomplish our ends. The stability of our labor is determined by the understructure. Not that which is seen makes us useful in God's plan but that which is unseen. Communion with Christ in some quiet retreat molds and fashions the life in His likeness and fits us to do His will among men.

Before Moses was fitted to deliver Israel he had to spend much time in the wilderness beside the burning bush. Before he was prepared to promulgate the divine law he tarried many days in the mount with God. So now we too should find some time to be alone with God. No day should pass without our heeding the call, "Come ye yourselves apart."

Let us not fail in this respect. Indeed, we must not fail if we would know the Lord, whom to know is life eternal.

The Washington *Star* made a wise observation on life today when it declared editorially that "what we need most is a renaissance of the ability to sit still." The great danger of these times is that men will demand action rather than thought. Modern man is in a hurry. He feels he has no time to lose. What has to be done must be done quickly. Who can take time to sit still? But the wise editor adds, "To men who have sat and thought we owe much."

The picture of a successful man today is one who is dashing here and there at as great speed as the latest inventions will allow him; one of quick and ready wit, who can give snap judgment on deals involving millions; one who, if he makes a mistake, will never acknowledge it, but will go on from where he failed to try some other course by a system of trial and error. But life is being run too much in this fashion, and the errors are too many.

All is not gain when we are in a constant state of activity. Neither is all loss when we take time to sit still. The great French banker and editor of an earlier day, Walter Bagehot, said, "It is certain that we should have been a far wiser race than we are if we had been readier to sit quiet. We should have known much better the way in which it was best to act when we come to act."

Men of more leisurely times than these felt the need of pause in the round of daily life. Lowell called solitude "the nurse of full-grown souls." And Wordsworth sounds almost modern in his plaintive verse:

> "When from our better selves we have too long
> Been parted by the hurrying world, and droop,
> Sick of its business, of its pleasures tired,
> How gracious, how benign, is Solitude."

The thing of first importance in life is to know God. And how shall we know Him? God answers that question. "Be still, and know that I am God."

This is not a plea for idleness and indifference. Far from it. It is rather a call for us to take time to consider the source of our wisdom and strength. The problems of life are growing more and more complicated. To solve one seems merely to create another. The distressed soul cries out, "What shall I do?" How comforting it is to know that we need not work out all the answers. If we will but sit still in quiet trust in God, many problems will disappear. Periods of hopeful meditation are necessary to real peace of heart and mind. Let us give Christ a chance to quiet the restless billows of our thoughts. Alone with God the things that have troubled us will not seem so important, and there we shall gain strength for the tasks that must be done. Yes, there beside still waters we shall refresh our souls. "When every other voice is hushed, and in quietness we wait before Him, the silence of the soul makes more distinct the voice of God. . . . Here alone can true rest be found."—*The Desire of Ages*, p. 363.